First World War
and Army of Occupation
War Diary
France, Belgium and Germany

58 DIVISION
Divisional Troops
290 Brigade Royal Field Artillery
1 October 1915 - 11 February 1916

WO95/2995/2

The Naval & Military Press Ltd
www.nmarchive.com
Published in association with The National Archives

Published by

The Naval & Military Press Ltd

Unit 10 Ridgewood Industrial Park,

Uckfield, East Sussex,

TN22 5QE England

Tel: +44 (0) 1825 749494

www.naval-military-press.com

www.nmarchive.com

This diary has been reprinted in facsimile from the original. Any imperfections are inevitably reproduced and the quality may fall short of modern type and cartographic standards.

© **Crown Copyright**
Images reproduced by permission of The National Archives, London, England, 2015.

Contents

Document type	Place/Title	Date From	Date To
Heading	WO95/2995-1		
Heading	58 Division Troops 290 Bde R F A. 1915 Oct-1916 Feb		
War Diary	Warren Heath	01/10/1915	31/10/1915
War Diary	Warren Heath Ipswich	06/11/1915	29/11/1915
War Diary	Warren Heath	02/12/1915	11/02/1916

WO 95/2995/1

58 DIVISION TROOPS

290 BDE RFA
(FORMERLY 2/1 LONDON BDE)

1915 OCT — 1916 FEB

Box 2995

290 BDE RFA (formerly 2/1 London) 2860

WAR DIARY

INTELLIGENCE SUMMARY

Army Form C. 2118

(Erase heading not required.)

LONDON DIVISION
GENERAL STAFF
2 - NOV. 1915

Place	Date	Hour	Summary of Events and Information	Remarks and references to Appendices
Warren Heath.	Oct 1		One Officer and 12 other ranks proceeded to Bordon to take over equipment, etc, of 1/1st London Brigade, R.F.A. (proceeding overseas).	
	" 10		Above party returned.	
	" 26		25 N.C.O's and men sent to Kettering to assist in looking after horses now being used by No.3 Training School. In addition to these, 1 Officer and 15 N.C.O's & men are still at Kettering awaiting leave to bring back horses, guns & equipment of 2/2nd Battery (taken over from 1/2nd Battery, gone overseas.)	
	" 30		61 Horses arrived from Remounts, Kettering.	
	" 31		12 " " " " Wembley.	
			150 " " " " Shirehampton.	

WARREN HEATH CAMP.
31st October 1915.

..................Colonel.
Comdg: 2/1st London Brigade, R.F.A.

Army Form C. 2118.

WAR DIARY
or
INTELLIGENCE SUMMARY
(Erase heading not required.)

Instructions regarding War Diaries and Intelligence Summaries are contained in F. S. Regs., Part II. and the Staff Manual respectively. Title pages will be prepared in manuscript.

Hour, Date, Place	Summary of Events and Information	Remarks and references to Appendices
Warren Heath, 6/11/15. Ipswich.	45 Horses arrived from Shirehampton.	
" 13/11/15.	33 Horses arrived from Avonmouth.	
" 20/11/15.	The following party returned from Kettering, after attachment to No. 3 Artillery Training School:- Captain S.H.Hurst, 4 N.C.O's, 34 men, 51 horses, 4 Guns & Limbers, 8 wagons & limbers, 1 Box Cart.	
" 29/11/15.	23 Ammunition Wagons. (18pr.) received from Barrow-in-Furness.	

Warren Heath Camp,
Ipswich,
30/11/15.

................Colonel.
Commanding
2/1st London Brigade, R.F.A.

Army Form C. 2118

WAR DIARY

INTELLIGENCE SUMMARY

(Erase heading not required.)

Instructions regarding War Diaries and Intelligence Summaries are contained in F. S. Regs., Part II. and the Staff Manual respectively. Title Pages will be prepared in manuscript.

Place	Date	Hour	Summary of Events and Information	Remarks and references to Appendices
Warren Heath	2/12/15		12 18-pr Q.F.Guns & Limbers arrived.	
	3/12/15		13 Wagons & Limbers arrived from Darnall Sheffield.	
	10/12/15		Brigade was inspected by Major General Brunker on Priory Heath.	
	25/12/15		Wire received during afternoon that air raid was expected.	
	28/12/15		Brigade was inspected by ~~Major~~ G.O.C. 58th London Division, on Martlesham Heath.	

Warren Heath Camp.

2/1/16

.... Colonel.

Comdg: 2/1st London Brigade, R.F.A.

Secret.

Army Form C. 2118

2/1st London Bde R.F.A.

WAR DIARY
INTELLIGENCE SUMMARY

(Erase heading not required.)

Instructions regarding War Diaries and Intelligence Summaries are contained in F.S. Regs., Part II. and the Staff Manual respectively. Title Pages will be prepared in manuscript.

Place	Date	Hour	Summary of Events and Information	Remarks and references to Appendices
Warren Heath.	4/1/16		4 15pr Guns & Limbers lent to 2/1st London R.G.A., Hadleigh.	
	7/1/16		2nd Lt L.A.G.Paine proceeded overseas to join 1st Line.	
	13/1/16		19 G.S.Wagons Mark X, arrived from Ordnance.	
			Lieut J.A.Davis proceeded overseas to join 1st Line.	
	14/1/16		4 15pr Guns & 8 Wagons, stores & ammunition, transferred to 2/A Bty H.A.C., Beepham.	
	15/1/16		4 do 8 -----do----- to 2/1st Berkshire R.H.A., Runcton.	
	19/1/16		2/3rd Battery left for Orford for Gun Practice on 20/1/16	
	20/1/16		2/1st -----do----- 21/1/16	
	21/1/16		2/2nd -----do----- 22/1/16	
	23/1/16	12-45 p.m.	Message received from D.H.Q. that a British Byplane would be proceeding between Southend Colchester, Ipswich and Norwich.	
	28/1/16	9-45 p.m.	Message received from Divl. Arty. H.Q. that a Zeppelin was reported, but no need for all ranks to turn out.	
	28/1/16		144,000 rds of .303 S.A.A. transferred to 1/8th Cyclist Battn, Essex Regt, Rayleigh (III Army)	
			144,000 -----do----- 2/8th " " " Gt Clacton (III Army)	
			Warren Heath Camp.	
			31.1.16.	
			O.Owen......Colonel.	
			Comdg: 2/1st London Brigade, R.F.A.	

SECRET.

Army Form C. 2118.

WAR DIARY
~~INTELLIGENCE SUMMARY~~

(Erase heading not required.)

Instructions regarding War Diaries and Intelligence Summaries are contained in F. S. Regs., Part II. and the Staff Manual respectively. Title pages will be prepared in manuscript.

Hour, Date, Place		Summary of Events and Information	Remarks and references to Appendices
Warren Heath.	February.		
	10th 3 p.m.	British byplane passed over camp from N.W. to S.E. flying low.	
	11th	4 15 pr Guns & Limbers returned from 2/1st London R.G.A., Hadleigh.	

Warren Heath Camp.
29. 2. 16.

..................Colonel.
Comdg: 2/1st London Brigade, R.F.A.